SCIENCE TRICKS & MAGIC

W9-BHF-403

Gaby Waters

Illustrated by
Graham Round

Designed by Kim Blundell

Contents

Science consultants
Julie Fitzpatrick and Alan Alder

About this book

In this book there are lots of
science tricks for you
to try on your friends. There
are also fun experiments with
strange results that make
science seem like magic.

All the experiments
are completely safe.

Some
experiments
are messy.

Try out
your tricks
on a willing
volunteer.

Some
experiments
are noisy.

You may need a grown
up to help you with
a few experiments.

The monster gang have tried
out every experiment. This
picture shows some of the
monsters at work.

Doing the experiments

The puzzle answers are on page 31.

The monsters show you how to do each experiment in easy step-by-step instructions.

You can find out how and why each experiment works. The scientific ideas behind each one are explained.*

There are ideas for further experiments to try and several science puzzles to solve.

Equipment and ingredients

All the experiments use ordinary, everyday equipment. You can probably find most of the ingredients at home. If not, you should be able to buy them at a local supermarket.

Yogurt cartons

Food coloring

Pins and nails

Paper clips

Thumbtacks

Kitchen matches

Clay

Corks

Magnets

Plastic bottles

It's a good idea to start collecting a science kit. Here are some things you may find useful.

*There are some extra, more detailed explanations on page 30.

Funny feelings

Snivel is doing some strange tests on his friends. He wants to find out how they feel things.

Find a willing test victim, and you can try them too. Compare your results with Snivel's.

The tweezer test

1

2 In some places Grummit can feel both prongs. In other places they feel like one.

3

4 Grummit's hands, especially his fingertips, are very sensitive.

I can feel 2 prongs.

First, Snivel blindfolds his friend Grummit to make sure he can't see anything.

He touches Grummit with a pair of tweezers (sometimes with 1 prong, sometimes with 2 prongs) and asks how many he can feel each time.

He marks each touch on a map of Grummit's body. Red dots stand for correct answers, blue dots for wrong answers.

Grummit's skin is most sensitive to touch in the places where he is able to feel 2 prongs.

How sensitive are your feet?

Many people, and all monsters, have very ticklish feet. But feet are not sensitive in the same way as fingertips. Try the tweezer test on the soles of your feet.

Snivel's touch detective game

The sensitive parts of your body are the parts with the best sense of touch. You can see this in Snivel's touch detective game.

First Snivel collects several different objects with varied shapes and surfaces.

He blindfolds Clutty Putty. She feels each object with her feet and tries to work out what it is.

Try it yourself – it's quite tricky. Then touch each object with your hands. See how much easier it is.

Feeling cold

Snivel is very very cold. He can't feel his fingertips and he is having trouble with the zipper of his ski suit.

He thinks that the cold has affected his sense of touch. Find out if he is right by trying the tests on the right.

Pinch-me test

Make one hand very cold. You could tie it to a bag of frozen peas or put it in a bowl of ice-cubes for a few minutes.

Ask someone to pinch one finger on each hand. Which one hurts most? Fumble's warm finger hurts much more than the cold one.

Pin test

Try picking up a pin with your cold hand. Fumble finds it very hard. The cold makes it difficult to feel the pin properly.

Eye tricks

Sometimes your eyes play tricks on you. They see things that are not really true. These are called optical illusions.

Look at the picture on the right. Slimy Sid thinks the red lines are curved. Is he correct?

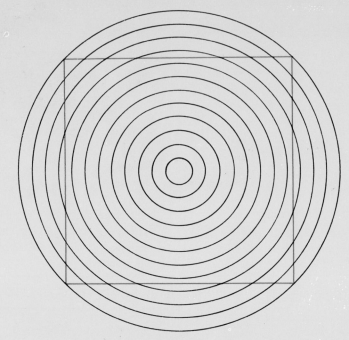

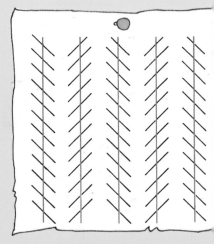

If you put a ruler along the red lines, you will see they are straight. Your eyes are fooled by the black circles which make the red lines seem curved.

Eye-teasers

Look first, then check what you see with a ruler. Did your eyes trick you?

Is the blue line longer than the green line, or are they the same length?

Are the green lines the same length or is the top one longer?

Are the red lines parallel? (Parallel lines are the same distance apart, all the way along.)

Color confusion

Colors can also fool your eyes. Light, bright colors can appear bigger than dark, dull colors. Light, bright colors reflect light whereas dark, dull colors swallow up or "absorb" light. Try the color trick, below, on your friends.

1 Draw round a glass to make a circle shape.

Cut out 2 paper circles exactly the same size. Paint one circle yellow and the other one dark brown.

2 The yellow circle looks bigger.

In fact they are the same size.

Stick the circles on a wall.* Tell your friends to go to the other end of the room. Ask them which circle looks bigger.

3 Which circle looks bigger?

Try the experiment again with other colors. You will probably find that light, bright colors seem larger than dark, dull ones.

Colored clothes

Some monsters think that dark colors make them look thin and light colors make them look fat.

Look around you and see if you think this is true.

*Check with a grown up first to make sure you don't damage the wall.

Magic bean stalks

The Gruesome twins have discovered that they can grow amazing plants from ordinary beans and seeds used for cooking and eating.

This picture shows some of the things they grew. They found everything in their kitchen cupboard.

Spice and herb seeds such as coriander, fennel and mustard seeds.

Dried peas and beans, such as kidney beans and butter beans.

Look for some beans and seeds in your own kitchen. You can find out how to grow them below.

How to grow seeds

Label each carton

Fester soaks the dried peas and beans in a bowl of water overnight. Then he buries them in cartons filled with soil. Blot sprinkles some of the small seeds on damp cotton. He plants others about a fingernail deep in the soil. They keep the soil and cotton damp and wait to see what will happen.

Some seeds grow tiny shoots in a day or two. Others grow very slowly and a few don't sprout at all. See what happens to your seeds.

Things to try

Some vegetables contain seeds. Try planting some.

Fester and Blot are having a fruit feast. As they eat the fruit, they plant the pips and stones. Try doing this yourself.

Slimy Sid is planting hamster food and bird seed. Aunty Mabel thinks he is silly. What do you think? Try it and see.

How seeds grow

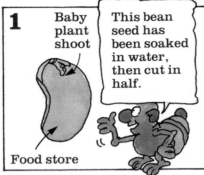

1

Baby plant shoot

This bean seed has been soaked in water, then cut in half.

Food store

A seed contains the beginnings of a baby plant and a store of food for the plant to use as it starts to grow.

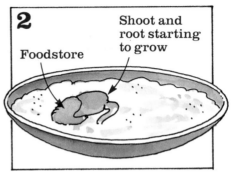

2

Foodstore

Shoot and root starting to grow

You can grow a seed on cotton because it has its own food store. Later the plant will make its own food.

3

A seed needs warmth and moisture to make it grow. Some seeds need a lot of warmth to start growing.

Did you know?

If seeds are kept dry, they will keep for ages without growing. In the desert, seeds lie in the ground until there is enough water to make them grow. After a rainfall lots of desert flowers appear.

4

If your seeds will not grow, try putting them in a warm place, such as a cupboard⋆

⋆Some seeds and beans that are meant for eating are treated to stop them growing.

Freaky flowers

You can fool your friends with freaky colored flowers, just like Slimy Sid's blue and green carnations.

To do this you will need a jar, food coloring, water and white flowers such as carnations.

How to do it

1 Pour some water and several drops of food coloring into the bottom of a jar. Put the flowers in the jar.

2 After a day or so, you will see flecks of color on the tips of the petals. In about 2 or 3 days the flowers change color completely.

1 DAY   3 DAYS

Why do the flowers change color?

Short-stemmed flowers change color faster than long-stemmed flowers. Can you guess why? Check your answer on page 31.

Flowers suck up water through their stems into their leaves and petals. You can't usually see this, but food coloring shows through white petals.

Plants in the soil

Plants suck up water from the soil through their roots and stems. The water contains minerals which the plants use to make food.

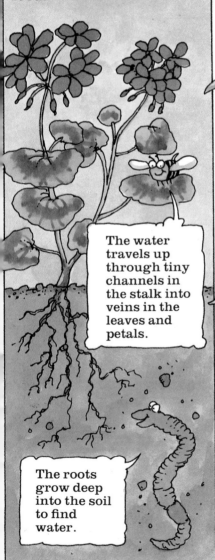

The water travels up through tiny channels in the stalk into veins in the leaves and petals.

The roots grow deep into the soil to find water.

Grummit's silly celery experiment

In some plants, such as celery, you can see the veins that carry water quite clearly. Try Grummit's silly celery experiment.

1

Grummit's assistant fills the bottom of a jar with water colored with food coloring. Grummit puts a stick of celery into the jar.

2

Grummit checks the celery every hour or so to watch the colored water creeping up the veins in the celery. His assistant makes a note of its progress.

3

Grummit cuts the celery into slices to see the veins more clearly. The spots of color show the ends of the veins.

Cooking magic

Snivel is doing some cooking. He is turning eggs, sugar and a little food coloring into monstrous blue meringues.

The monster gang think it might be magic, but Snivel says it is science. Follow Snivel's recipe and see what you think.

Is it magic?

2½ hours later, the gooey swirls have turned into crisp meringues. Find out how this happens, below.

When you whisk egg whites, hundreds of tiny air bubbles get trapped and make a stiff foam.

The oven's heat makes the air bubbles "expand" and the foam puffs up. It also causes a chemical change in the egg white making it solid. This is called "coagulation".

1

Snivel asks Aunty Mabel to turn the oven to 225°F/110°C or gas mark ¼.

2

This is quite tricky

He separates the whites from the yolks of 4 eggs. You can ask a grown-up to help you do this.

3

He whisks the egg whites in a big bowl. First they go fluffy, then they go stiff and white.

4

When the egg white is stiff, Snivel adds 220g (8oz) of superfine sugar and stirs it in very gently. Weedle adds a few drops of food coloring.

5

He drops spoonfuls of the mixture in round, swirly shapes on to greased baking trays. He puts them in the oven for 2½ hours.

12

Cooking cake mixture

The heat in an oven turns a sticky mixture of butter, sugar, eggs and flour into a cake.

The heat dries out some of the liquid in the mixture.

Heat hardens a substance called gluten in the flour and turns the egg white solid.

Tiny air bubbles in the cake mixture expand. This makes the cake "rise" and gives it a light and fluffy texture.

Deadeye Dick's dreadful disaster

My cake is flat.

Deadeye Dick's cake is a disaster. It hasn't risen. He followed the recipe correctly, but he kept opening the oven door while it was cooking. Can you guess what went wrong? Check your answer on page 31.

More about eggs

Ask a grown-up to help you poach or fry an egg. Watch it coagulate (turn from a liquid into a solid). Which part of the egg goes solid first?

In a very hot climate, eggs can coagulate in the heat of the sun.

Tricks with shadows

The monster gang are enthralled by Deadeye Dick's Magical Shadow Show. Follow what they are doing in the picture on the right, and you can make a shadow show too.

For moving puppets, make shapes with your hands.

For the screen, you can use a white wall or white paper stuck to a bulletin board.

You need a flashlight with a bright beam.

The room should be completely dark.

To make shadow puppets, cut shapes and figures out of cardboard and stick them to long, thin sticks.

Scary shadows

On dark and eerie nights, Slimy Sid scares his friends with spooky shadows at the windows. You can find out how he does it, below.

1

First he sticks white paper on the outside of a window. He stands back and shines a flashlight on it.

2

Then his assistant makes monstrous, scary movements in front of the flashlight's beam.

3

Inside, in the dark, the monsters see a spooky shadow moving against a ghostly, light window.

14

How shadows are made

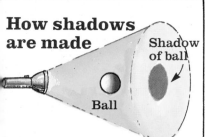

Shadow of ball

Ball

Shadows are made when light is blocked by an object. Light travels in lots of straight lines called rays. Light rays cannot bend round things that get in their way. Objects that block light are said to be "opaque".

Making shadows bigger

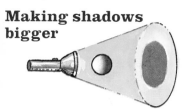

Bring the flashlight closer to the object. It blocks more light, so its shadow is bigger.

Making shadows smaller

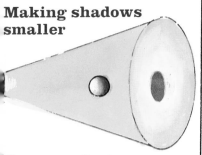

Now move the flashlight away. The shadow gets smaller because it blocks less of the light.

Mystery shadows

Transparent (see-through) objects cast only very faint shadows. This is because most of the light rays can travel through them. Snivel is making some weird, mystery shadows with transparent objects.

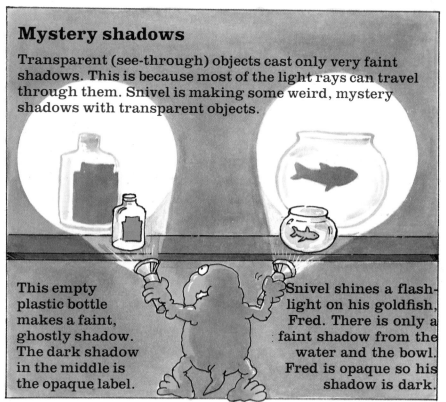

This empty plastic bottle makes a faint, ghostly shadow. The dark shadow in the middle is the opaque label.

Snivel shines a flashlight on his goldfish, Fred. There is only a faint shadow from the water and the bowl. Fred is opaque so his shadow is dark.

Shadow puzzle

Grummit is at the monster cup final (Monster Gang Utd v Reptile Rangers). He can't work out why each player has 4 shadows. Can you? Check your answer on page 31.

Magical magnets

Magnets have a strange power. They pull things towards them, as if by magic.

You can find out about magnets and this peculiar power below. Then try some of the monsters' favorite magnet tricks and games, on the right.

Bar magnets

Horseshoe magnets

These magnets come from the inside of old loudspeakers.

These are fun magnets for sticking onto metal surfaces.

Magnets come in all sorts of shapes and sizes. You can buy them in toy shops, hardware shops and department stores.

To find out if something is magnetic, hold a magnet close to it.

Magnets pull or "attract" most (but not all) metal things. When something is attracted by a magnet it is said to be magnetic.

The pull of the magnet is strongest at its ends.

You can feel the pull of a magnet when you hold a nail or pin close to it. Which part of the magnet pulls hardest?

Some magnets have a stronger pulling force than others.

Slimy Sid's magnetic mini-monsters

Slimy Sid terrifies his Aunty Mabel with his magnetic mini-monsters. You can make your friends squeal and squirm too. Find out how on the right.

Magnet puzzles

See if you can solve these two puzzles. You can check your solutions on page 31.

1

2

Can you remove a paper clip from a glass of water? You can't put anything in the glass nor can you tip out the water.

Slimy Sid has dropped Aunty Mabel's pins and plastic buttons. He has 30 seconds to sort them out and pick them up. How can he do it?

Make a small monster shape out of clay. Stick a thumbtack into the bottom.

The magnet attracts the metal thumbtack through the tray.

Magnet

Put the monster on a tray and hold a magnet under it, below the monster. Move the magnet and the monster should move too.*

If you attach a magnet to a long stick, you can control your monster from a distance.

Sharks and shrimps

Try playing Sharks and Shrimps. Cut out lots of paper shrimps and 6 paper sharks. Attach a paper clip to each one and put them in a box.

Shark   Shrimp

The players fish for shrimps with a magnet tied to a piece of string. The winner is the one to catch the most shrimps. If you catch a shark, you're out.

More about magnets

The ends of a magnet are called poles. One is a north pole, the other a south pole. If you have two magnets, try holding the ends together.

If the ends pull together it means one is a north pole and other is a south pole.

If they push away or "repel" each other, it means they are both the same type.

Something to try

If you float a bar magnet in a bowl of water, one end will point to the North. This is why the ends of a magnet are called north and south poles.

Float the magnet in a plastic container.

*If the monster doesn't move very well, try a stronger magnet or a thinner tray.

17

Disappearing tricks

Deadeye Dick has discovered a way of making things disappear. To try out his tricks you need a color viewer. Find out how to make one on the right.

> You could use a cellophane candy wrapper, like this.

1 Find a piece of yellow cellophane or clear yellow plastic.

2 Cut out a cardboard frame, just bigger than the cellophane.

3 Stick the cellophane to the frame with glue or tape.

Vanishing windows

> Some of the windows have disappeared! Now there are only 17.

This is a picture of Pessky Mo's new igloo. There are 21 windows. Look at the igloo through your yellow viewer and count the number of windows again.

Why the windows disappear

The yellow viewer makes the white walls look yellow. The yellow windows do not show up against the walls and so they "disappear".

Try making a red viewer. Look at the picture again. How many windows are there now?

Magical mystery message

Copy this message on to a sheet of white paper. Write the ringed letters in yellow and each of the others in a different color. Read the message through your yellow viewer.

NO (SMOKING)(IS) ALLOWED IN THE (T)RAIN

The yellow letters should disappear and change the message.

Perhaps you can invent some mystery messages of your own.

How color viewers work

Light looks colorless, but really it is made up of different colors. You can sometimes see these colors in rainbows.

A color viewer separates or "filters" the colors in light. It only lets light the same color as itself travel through it.

Try looking through different color viewers.

Color viewers, or filters, make white things appear the same color as themselves, but they can also change other colors.

Snivel's red viewer only lets through red light. Slimy Sid's white bow tie look red, but his green body looks black!

Slimy Sid's car crash puzzle

Slimy Sid has just had an unfortunate collision with a monster-police car. He says he didn't see the red light. Can you work out why? Check your answer on page 31.

Musical magic

The monster gang are making magic musical sounds with everyday objects. Try doing this yourself.

Try making sounds with other ordinary things you find about the house, too.

Tap a blunt table knife. Listen to the humming sound it makes.

Wobble a large piece of stiff cardboard backwards and forwards.

Hang a saucepan lid or knives and forks on a string. Tap them with a metal spoon.

Gently rub a damp finger round and round the rim of a wine glass. It should produce a strange singing sound.

Ask a grown up to bend a saw backwards and forwards. It makes an almost spooky sound. Don't try this yourself.

How sounds are made

All sounds are caused by shaking movements called vibrations.

Ordinary everyday objects produce sounds when they are made to vibrate.

You can see the blade vibrating in a blur of movement.

When an object vibrates it makes the air around it vibrate as well. The vibrations travel

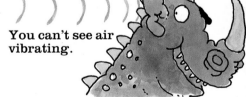

You can't see air vibrating.

through the air. Your ear drum shakes with the vibration and you hear a sound.

Changing speed

You can make a sound higher or lower by changing the speed or "frequency" of a vibration. A fast vibration makes a high note. A slow vibration makes a low note.

You can test this out by wobbling a piece of cardboard at different speeds.

Try plucking a rubber band. Then stretch it and pluck it again. It vibrates more quickly when it is stretched and the plucking sound is higher.

Slimy Sid's piano trick

Slimy Sid sings a note into the open top of the piano and presses the loud pedal (the one on the right). The monster gang are amazed. The piano "sings" the same note back to him, as if by magic. If you have a piano, you can try it yourself.

What is happening?

The piano string that makes the same note as Slimy Sid vibrates in sympathy. This is called resonance.

Aunty Mabel's singing wine glass

Aunty Mabel is trying to make a wine glass resonate. Follow what she does and try it yourself.

It is very hard to do this.

1 Aunty Mabel pings a wine glass with her nail to find out what note it makes.

2 Then she tries to sing the same note. If she succeeds, the glass should resonate.

3 If her voice is loud enough, the glass could vibrate so much that it cracks.

Clutty Putty's purple potion

The monster gang are puzzled by Clutty Putty's purple potion. When it mixes with another ingredient it changes color, as if by magic.

Color changes

Clutty puts a little purple potion in the bottom of 2 small jars. She pours a teaspoon of vinegar into the jar on the left and a teaspoon of baking powder into the jar on the right.

You can discover the secret of how and why it works on the opposite page. First find out how to make it, below.

How to make the potion

1
Chop up half a red cabbage. Put the pieces in a saucepan and cover them with cold water.

2
Put the saucepan on the stove and let it boil for 5 minutes. Ask a grown up to help you do this.

3
When it is cool, separate the cabbage and the liquid by straining it through a sieve.*

Almost immediately the liquid changes color. In the jar on the left, the potion turns pink, on the right it turns green.

*You need the liquid, not the cabbage bits. You can eat these if you like.

Why the potion changes color

The purple potion is an indicator. It changes color when it mixes with an acid or an alkali. These are names scientists use to describe and group substances.

Vinegar is an acid. It turns the potion pink. Baking powder is an alkali and it turns the potion green.

Milk

Fizzy cola

Lime juice

Tooth paste

Laundry soap

Yogurt

Salt   Soap

Black tea

Lemon juice

Baking powder

You can record the results of each test in a notebook.

Lime juice   Green   Acid

Here are some everyday acid and alkali substances. See if you can sort out the acids from the alkalis. Follow what Snivel does on the right.

Snivel puts some of each substance into a little purple potion. Acids turn the potion red or pink. Alkalis turn the potion green or blue.

Mixing acids with alkalis

Guess what happens to the purple potion if you mix it with an acid and an alkali at the same time. Try it and see.

1

2

Mix a little lemon juice (acid) with some purple potion and it should turn pink. Add some laundry soap (alkali) to the mixture. It should turn back to purple. This means that the mixture is neither acid nor alkali. In other words, it is neutral.

Did you know?

Bee sting poison is acid. You can soothe bee stings by rubbing them with bicarbonate of soda (an alkali).

23

Balancing tricks

Have you ever tried walking
along a narrow wall or
plank with your arms
pinned to your sides?
This is what the
monsters
are trying
to do. It's
very tricky.
Try it
yourself.

If your hands
leave the side of
your body, you
must start again.

It is much easier to walk
with your arms stretched out. You balance
more easily because your body makes a wider
shape and your weight is spread out over your feet.

More about balancing

When something balances, it is said to be stable. This means
it is hard to topple over. Low things with a wide base are
more stable than tall things with a narrow base.

Some of these objects are more stable than others. Which are
they? Try knocking them over to find out.

Making things stable

You can make something
more stable by giving it a
broader base. Try sticking
a piece of cardboard to the
bottom of a cardboard tube.
It is more difficult
to push over.

Another way of making
something more stable it
to make its base heavier.
Pour some water into a
plastic bottle. It should
topple over less easily.

Balancing puzzles

Aunty Mabel's automobile

Blot's buggy

Snivel's speed machine

Which of these monster vehicles is the most stable? You can check your answer on page 31.

Which boat is more likely to topple over and capsize?

Balancing potato monster

1

It will not stand up on its own.

Make a monster out of a knobbly potato. Give it matchstick arms and legs and drawing pin eyes.

2 Curve the wire like this.

Stick a length of stiff wire into the potato. Attach another, larger potato to the other end.

3

Put the monster on a shelf and it should balance, wobbling backwards and forwards.

How does it balance?

The potato monster balances because the greatest part of its weight (the second potato) comes below the point where it balances (its matchstick feet).

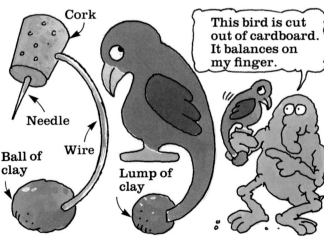

Cork

Needle

Ball of clay

Wire

Lump of clay

This bird is cut out of cardboard. It balances on my finger.

These toys balance in the same way. Try making them.

Tricky reflections

A reflection is what you see when you look in a mirror. You can also see reflections in water, windows and other shiny surfaces.

Like most monster magicians, Slimy Sid uses reflections to create special effects. Try his finger in the flame trick, on the right.

1

Flame's reflection

Flame

To set the trick up, Slimy Sid puts a lighted candle in front of a window. The flame is reflected in the window.

2

Unlit candle

He goes outside with an unlit candle. Weedle tells him where to stand so the unlit candle appears below the reflection.

3

Slimy Sid puts his finger on the unlit candle wick. The monsters come into the room and see his finger in the flame!

Slimy Sid's Super Snooper

Slimy Sid's Super Snooper uses mirrors to peep round corners and spy over the fence. Try making one yourself.

Things you need

Piece of cardboard 55cm (22in) long and 35cm (14in) wide, 2 pocket mirrors about 9cm (3½in) long and 6cm (2½in) wide, scissors, glue and tape.

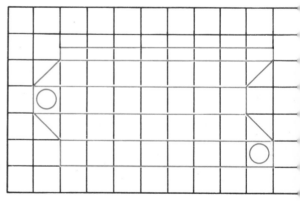

1

Draw lines on the cardboard to make a grid, as above. Space the lines exactly 5cm (2in) apart. Copy the red and green lines and the red circles on to your grid.

Mirror tricks

You can do strange tricks with mirrors because reflections show things back to front.

Lopside Ed's reflection is different from his passport photo.

Put a patch over your left eye. Look at your reflection. Which eye is covered?

Try holding this book in front of the mirror. Why can't you read it?

Car puzzle

Slimy Sid has copied the monster ambulance by painting a back to front sign on his car. Do you know why?*

Cut around the red lines. Then cut out the red circles to make two holes.

Fold the cardboard on the green lines to make a square tube. Stick down the flap.

Mirror

Attach a mirror (reflective side facing inwards) to each end of the tube.

How it works

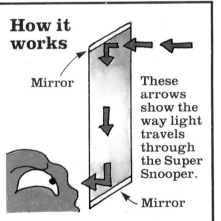

Mirror

These arrows show the way light travels through the Super Snooper.

Mirror

The mirror at the top reflects light down the tube. The mirror at the bottom reflects the light into your eye.

Sinking and floating

Deadeye Dick has promised a trip on his racing raft to the first monster who can make a lump of clay float.

The monster gang are not having much luck. See if you can do it. There are some clues about how things float, below.

How things float

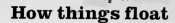

1 When you put something in water, some of the water is pushed aside, or "displaced". Slimy Sid's bath overflows because his body displaces the water.

2 Big things displace more water than small things. Ugly Mug has a bigger body than Slimy Sid, so he displaces more water.

3 You can feel upthrust in a swimming pool. Stretch out your arms and they float upwards.

When water is displaced, a force called "upthrust" pushes upwards. The amount of upthrust depends on how much water is displaced.

4 This clay lump sinks. It is quite heavy but it is small and doesn't displace much water. This means there is not enough upthrust to make it float.

Slimy Sid's magic egg trick

Slimy Sid puts an egg into a jar filled with water. It sinks.

He puts the same egg into another jar. Magically, it floats.

How the trick works

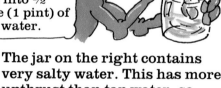

To make salty water, stir about 8 tablespoons of salt into ½ litre (1 pint) of hot water.

The jars contain different types of water. Different types of water have different amounts of upthrust. The jar on the left contains tap water.

The jar on the right contains very salty water. This has more upthrust than tap water, so things float in it more easily.

Did you know?

On the high seas

On Reptile River

There is more upthrust in sea water than there is in river water. This means that Deadeye Dick's pirate ship, the Jolly Dodger, floats higher in the salty sea than it does on the Reptile River.

5

Mould the clay into a bowl shape. It is still as heavy as the lump, but it is bigger and displaces more water. This means there is more upthrust and it floats.

Further explanations

The explanations in this book are obviously highly simplified. The notes below are intended for those who wish to explain the activities in more detail, to older children.

Pages 16-17

Magnets attract iron and steel and alloys that contain these metals. Magnets do not point to the geographical north pole. Instead, they point to a position in Northern Canada called the magnetic north pole.

Pages 18-19

Light is made up of a mixture of colors. These are commonly divided into 7 colors of the spectrum: red, orange, yellow, green, blue, indigo and violet.

Objects appear colored because of the color of light they reflect. For instance, a red object reflects red light, but it absorbs all the other colors. A white object reflects all the colors of light. A black object absorbs them.

A color filter allows light the same color as itself to pass through it. For instance, a green filter permits green light to pass through it but it blocks other colors. If you look at a red object through a green filter, its red light is blocked. No light passes through the filter and so the object appears black.

There are three primary colors of light: red, green and blue. Other colors are a mixture of these. They act differently to colored paints. For instance, green and red paint make brown, but green and red light make yellow.

If you look at a yellow object through a green filter, it appears green. This happens because the red light reflected by the yellow object is blocked, but the green light is allowed through.

Pages 20-21

Vibrations force the surrounding air to vibrate by pushing the air molecules together, forming a compression. The compression is passed on through the air in a wave.

The pitch of a sound depends on how frequent vibrations are. The number of vibrations made in 1 second is called frequency and is measured in Hertz (Hz). The human ear can usually hear sounds with frequencies between 20 vibrations per second (20Hz) and 20,000 vibrations per second (20kHz).

Pages 22-23

Clutty Putty's purple potion is a well known home-made indicator. An indicator is used to show the presence of acid or alkali in a substance.

Chemists use a range of numbers (called pH numbers) to measure levels of acidity and alkalinity. Acids range from 1 to 6, alkalis from to 14 and 7 is neutral.

Pages 24-25

Balance depends on the pull of the earth's gravity. Gravity pulls downwards on every particle of an object with a force that is equal to the weight of the particle. At the same time, there is a point where the whole weight of an object seems to act and it balances. This is called the center of gravity.

Stable objects have a low center of gravity: the lower the center of gravity, the greater the stability. The center of gravity can be lowered by widening the base or increasing the weight of the base.

An object always tries to move until its center of gravity is as low as possible. In other words it will topple over. This is what happens if you try to balance a pencil on its point.

An object topples over when its center of gravity moves outside its base. This explains why it is difficult to walk along a narrow wall with your arms pinned to your sides. If you hold your arms out and move them up and down, you can alter your center of gravity to keep it above, not outside, your base (your feet).

Pages 26-27

A light ray reflects or bounces off a plane (flat) mirror at the same angle as it hits it.

Slimy Sid's super snooper is a periscope. The mirrors are tilted at 45°. The light rays hit the first mirror at 45° and bounce off at the same angle. This means they effectively turn a corner to travel at right angles down the tube. The same thing happens at the second mirror, but in the opposite direction. The light rays hit the mirror at 45° and bounce off at the same angle, out of the periscope into your eye.

Pages 28-29

The amount of upthrust on an object in a liquid is equal to the weight of the liquid the object displaces. An object displaces the same volume of liquid in salt water as it does in fresh water. But salt water is denser (heavier) than fresh water. This means the upthrust in salt water is greater.

Puzzle answers

Page 10

Short-stemmed flowers change color more quickly because the colored water has less distance to travel to the petals.

Page 13

Deadeye Dick's cake is flat because he opened the oven door while it was cooking. This let cold air into the oven which stopped the air bubbles puffing up, or expanding.

Page 15

The players have 4 shadows because of the floodlights. There are 4 sets of floodlights, one in each corner of the field. Each set casts a separate shadow.

Page 16

1. Hold a magnet under the glass, then slide it gently up the side. The magnet should be strong enough to pull the paper clip with it.
2. Slimy Sid should hold a magnet over the pins and buttons. The magnet will pick up the metal pins but not the plastic buttons. (He will have to pick up the buttons by hand.)

The green lenses in Slimy Sid's glasses only let through green light. They block the color of the red traffic light. To Slimy Sid, the red light would look black.

Page 25

1. Snivel's speed machine is the most stable. It has a wide base and the weight is low.
2. The Slime family are standing up which makes their boat top heavy and likely to capsize. Deadeye Dick's boat is more stable. He is sitting down which keeps the weight in the boat low.

Page 27

The sign on Slimy Sid's car will read correctly when the driver in front looks into the rear-view mirror, attached to the windshield.

Ambulances use back to front signs to tell drivers what sort of vehicle is coming up behind. A driver reads the word AMBULANCE and gets out of the way in an emergency.

Index

First published in 1985 by Usborne Publishing Ltd, 20 Garrick Street, London WC2E 9BJ, England.

© 1985 Usborne Publishing Ltd.

The name Usborne and the device 🙂 are the Trade Marks of Usborne Publishing Ltd.

American Edition 1986
Printed in Belgium.